May God DEFINE all your moments!

Kel Rolly

Proverbs 3:5,6

Defining Moments

Overflowing with Living Words

Kel Rohlf

Defining Moments Overflowing with Living Words

No part of this publication may be reproduced in any form or by any means without the written permission of the author; except by a reviewer, who may quote brief passages for a review.

Every reasonable attempt has been made to identify owners of copyright. Errors or corrections will be corrected in subsequent editions.

Copyright © by Kel Rohlf 2011

ISBN: 978-0-9837696-8-2

Library of Congress Control Number: 2011940605

Cover Art by Mary Heinze © 2011

Scriptures taken from the Holy Bible,
  New International Version®, NIV®.
  Copyright © 1973, 1978, 1984 by Biblica, Inc.™
  Used by permission of Zondervan.
  All rights reserved worldwide.
  www.zondervan.com

Printed in the United States of America
No Waste Publishing
www.nowastepublishing.com

For El-Shaddai—

LORD God Almighty,

Father, Son and Holy Spirit

My Sustainer, My Strength, My Sustenance

My All in All

My Song, My Salvation, My Sunshine

My Friend— Jesus

Table of Contents

Apt	1
Beloved	5
Blessed	9
Change	13
Choose	18
Clarity	21
Cram	25
Cure	28
Define	31
Deliver	35
Ending	39
Epiphany	42
Expect	45
Focus	48
Gospel	50
Home	54
Hope	57
Husbandry	60
Journey	64
Love	67
New	70
Persevere	73
Residue	77
Resist	81
Retreat	86
Root	89
Sabotage	91
Surrender	95

Time	98
Unruly	101
Walk	104
Wet	107

Preface

Defining Moments: Overflowing with Living Words is a collection of musings upon life and how words lead to deeper meaning. When I feel lost, bored or uncertain of what life means I run to my dictionary. The flow of definitions sharpens my focus and realigns my perspective. The other place I find refuge is in the Word, not just Scriptures, but the person of Jesus Christ, my Lord and Savior.

Ever since I decided to follow Jesus when I was a young girl, He has been leading me on one adventure after another. Over the years I have become a more fervent follower. I weathered the teen years in the midst of family upheaval, as well as navigating all the other passages of growing up.

Jesus loves me, a simple, but true statement. This one truth imbues all of my defining moments. I pray that as you read these pages, glimpses of His steadfast love will bring light to the dark recesses of your heart, giving you hope and joy.

I would like to thank Gloria Baraks, Marijo Blair and the writer's group at First Evangelical Free Church of Manchester, Missouri, for their valuable feedback and encouragement over the years. Special thanks to Jeanette Findley, Tracy Flori, Kelly Greer, Carol Grimmer, Mary Heinze, Robyn Lyster, and my aunt Esther Thompson for reading and proofreading these offerings. Without their help and support, this book would not have been born. Also many thanks to my friends who have read these devotions over the years, when I used to send them out in a group e-mail. Your timely words of encouragement and testimony of receiving them just when you needed them kept me writing. Your interest helped me to keep my eyes open for the defining moments of life.

Much love and gratitude overflows to my husband, Les Rohlf, for all his support and sacrifice to make this dream come true. I am ever grateful for the gift of our companionship and love. Out of this love was born two wonderful young men, Kurtis and Bradley—you're the best! Thanks for sharing life with me.

Before a word is on my tongue
you know it completely, O LORD.
Psalm 139:4

Apt
unusually fitted or qualified[1]

> *A man finds joy in giving an apt reply —*
> *and how good is a timely word!*
> *Proverbs 15:23*

Apt is a nice little word containing a depth of meaning. After recently studying the spiritual disciplines, I challenged myself to choose one that held particular meaning for me and then to practice it. In my journal I posed the following question: *Which discipline is apt for this life season?*

I don't know why, but the word apt has a nice ring to it, and my curious little mind had to know what it really meant. So I looked up its definition with one of my favorite companions: the dictionary.

With the definition in mind, I continued my contemplation of pursuing God through a certain spiritual discipline. As I thought about the meaning of apt, another question surfaced. Does this approach to God fit my personality and particular circumstances? Am I well fitted for solitude and silence, or is service and celebration more my tendency? Am I inclined to fast and pray, or am I more likely to begin a regimen of study that leads to times of meditation?

I wanted to not only participate in the spiritual disciplines that were most suited to me, but also to learn which ones I would most ordinarily be disposed to, so that when struggling with a sense of distance, or wondering will I ever "hear" from God again, I could run to Him through that discipline which best fastened my soul to His heart.

After I had my side trip into the dictionary, my thoughts returned to my original question. "Which discipline is apt for this life season?" As I thought about this, I had a defining moment. "Study, that's it!" In light of my love for learning and my new adventure of taking classes at college, I decided study would be the discipline to pursue.

In my journal I came across a prayer written during the time I had been weighing the decision to go back to school:

> *May the discipline of study, whether spiritual or academic lead me to a deeper knowledge of God that is marked by humility, not arrogance.*

The desire to study and contemplate God was evident, yet I was concerned that I might fall into a performance trap that would lead to pride, rather than heart knowledge. Much of my childhood esteem was garnered through doing well in school. I was quite the performer; I remember the smugness of being called forward several times at the award ceremonies to receive my certificate of excellence in each subject. A lot of my esteem still centers on whether or not I do well.

God reminds me over and over that He is not evaluating my performance record, but my heart. This is so freeing. I believe God enjoys the "work" we each accomplish in His power and for His glory. He cares about everything we are involved in. During this season of life I decided to pursue study to engage my entire person in the pursuit of loving God and others.

What joy we find, when we are in a position to be responsive to God and His words. To enjoy the pursuit of knowing God more intimately, we must have a keen intellect and be responsive to that which God conveys to each of us. It is good that God designed us with multiple capacities to express and experience the lavish love He offers, and that He longs to receive in return.

Since returning to school I found it more difficult to find extended time to delve into God's word. So I dug out a couple of devotional CDs and began listening to them on my commute to school, which turned out to be an "apt reply and timely word."

With the routine of going to school, I hoped to meet God the same way, the same time and same location each day. My success with this type of plan often ends in discouragement. Ever so gently through the message on the CD, He reminded me that He wants to be my Friend and He actually desires me to interact with Him in various ways; in fact, He delights in my tendency toward variety, spontaneity and creativity. My self-inflicted performance test of meeting with God in a certain way was put aside once again. Later that week I realized that I had connected with God in many ways, except for the ways I had prescribed for myself. God is committed to relationship; for that I am ever grateful.⚜

Beloved
dearly loved; dear to the heart[2]

*Let the morning bring me word of your unfailing love,
for I have put my trust in you. Show me the way I should
go, for to you I lift up my soul.*
Psalm 143:8

To *be* loved, that is what we long for. So many things happen throughout our lives that we may begin to feel unloved. My experience has been to correlate this feeling of being unloved with a specific person in my life. From a very young age I learned that God loved me so much that He gave up His only begotten Son. So, I think it is easier to blame others for my pain, instead of voicing my real questions: Do you really love me, God? If so, then why so many hard things? Why death? Why sickness? Why distance?

I am not going to even try to answer for God here. But I think it is important for me to voice these questions, just like Job did, and be open to God's response (Job 42:1-6). I am humbled by God's grace, which allows me to pour out my complaints. Then He sets me straight. After that He encourages me to remember the ways He has always loved me. And when I'm open to it, I experience His love in tangible ways.

Let me tell you a couple ways I have experienced his tangible love this past year. The amazing thing is that God actually demonstrated this one example twice. This year I volunteered with the receptions after the spring and winter concerts at the middle school. One of my tasks for both concerts was to order and pick up corsages and boutonnieres for the directors. When I went to pick up the ones for Christmas, I thought how lovely it would be to receive a corsage. As I looked over the order, I realized they had an extra corsage. The florist said I could have it. When I got back in my car the tears flowed, as I gratefully realized my heavenly Father had heard my heart's desire.

The spring has been particularly difficult with many episodes of loss for me and my family, and others around me. My step-father passed away in April. Very soon after that we got a call that my Dad had been admitted to the hospital. It's difficult to help when you live so far away, indeed, I couldn't help except through prayers and phone calls. So last weekend, I had a good cry and lashing out at God, who wondrously remained silent.

On Mother's Day, it was as if God had tailored the sermon at church directly to some of my questions. The title was "When God is Silent". Once again God was reassuring me of His love and interest in my life. I had a nice day with my family, and then took my mom to lunch on the spur of the moment. She and I talked about longing to cherish the moments we have now.

In the midst of the grief and pain, I had another round of corsages to pick up that Monday afternoon. The sales lady asked me what event the flowers were for. I said for a school concert. Are you going she inquired? As I replied, yes, she went over to the flower case and handed me a corsage. She said I could have it, as it was leftover from Mother's Day. Once again in the car, I just sobbed as the tangible steadfast love of God flooded my heart. I wore it that evening. Everyone who asked about the corsage, I told my story. I made sure they knew it was a gift from God. Some may think it was a coincidence that I got the first corsage, but I am very certain that both times my heavenly Father was intentionally saying, "I love you!"

We all have insecurity attacks, especially when life seems to be crumbling around us. We all have a desire for unfailing love, yet one of the ways that we often insulate ourselves from love occurs through deceiving ourselves. We tell ourselves one of two things: one, I don't really need love. Or two, I will find love my own way. If we take those paths, we'll never catch those glimpses of divine love.

If we say our greatest need is anything other than unfailing love, we are deceiving ourselves. In Scripture, the thirty-two times that unfailing love is used it is in reference to the quality of God's love. Beloved, is an endearing term. We are His beloved.∽

Blessed

bringing pleasure, contentment, or good fortune[3]

> *Blessed are the pure in heart,*
> *for they will see God.*
> *Matthew 5:8*

Blessed is a word more often than not associated with people of the Bible. The covenant that God made initially with Abraham included hopeful words that extend to us today (Genesis 12:2-3). This promise indicated that all peoples would one day be blessed through a descendant of Abraham. All indications point to Jesus as being the fulfillment of this promise.

Most people I know want to be blessed or live a life that is marked by blessing. We long for happiness, joy and bliss. We want rewards and favor. At the end of Abraham's life the author states this about his life: "and the LORD had blessed him in every way" (Genesis 24:1b). Isn't that what we want as well? Yet a blessed life indicates a consecrated life. The consecrated life may be marked by sacrifice, yet it is only attainable through the benefits bestowed on followers of

Christ. He has given us the purpose, the power and plan to live consecrated lives.

The purpose has been predetermined. The power is experienced through His personal involvement with us through the indwelling Holy Spirit. The plan is outlined in Scriptures. The Magna Carta of Blessedness can be found in Jesus' teaching found in the Beatitudes (Matthew 5:1-10). Jesus in this teaching tells us that blessedness is an inward condition. I want to focus on two specific principles for blessedness. Both are natural conditions that we experience as we live out life. We hunger and thirst daily, and we face grief and loss constantly.

Hunger and thirst are daily conditions, in which we find ourselves. Jesus whets our appetite for the spiritual by comparing it to a common, strong urge of our humanness. We can all relate to experiencing hunger and thirst. I love how He relates this physical need to our spiritual need for righteousness. The concept of righteousness is truly something we all want to comprehend. I want to get it right, don't you? Even before someone tells me that something is incorrect, there's an innate desire to get it right. I didn't go to school and say I hope I get the answers wrong; in fact, there was penalty for getting it wrong. If I'm venturing into a new unexplored area of life, I want to find out how to approach it in a way that will not produce failure. Spiritually, and even morally we want what is right. The promise to the one who hungers and thirsts for righteousness is fulfillment. This is something that God wants to satisfy in us. He wants to lead us into right living. We cannot give ourselves righteousness, but God did create us with an appetite for it, which is fulfilled and satisfied in relationship with Jesus (1 Corinthians 1:30; 2 Corinthians 5:21).

Last year as I was going through some soul searching, as well as struggling with discouragement and even some depression. The following statement became my meditation, "Blessed are those who mourn, for they will be comforted" (Matthew 5:4). I wondered why this verse came to me during a time of undefined sadness in my life, rather than on the occasion of physical loss. I wondered how mourning could be a blessing. It was simple, yet profound. The blessing would be found in mourning over the sadness of life changes, of disappointing relationships and of transitioning from a mother of toddlers to teenagers. (I know this didn't happen overnight, but last year I felt like it did.) Unless one mourns, how can they be comforted?

I was not allowing myself to grieve, nor coming to Jesus with my pain; I was just trying to figure it out. Talking, complaining or explaining to whoever was on my path, so I could feel better.

But ever so gently, I kept hearing the invitation to mourn. Mourn and I will comfort you; a promise that Jesus faithfully keeps. Mourn and you will be released into blessing. The discouragement will be named. The depression will lift in due time, but in the meantime grieve. In some miraculous way grief gives way to joy and to restored hope.

Another Scripture that led me out of the darkness was this treasure: "Hope deferred makes the heart sick, but a longing fulfilled is a tree of life" (Proverbs 13:12). Denying hope, smothering it with despair leads to heartache, but confessing our desires and going to the One who longs to fulfill them is like returning to Eden, to the place where we were intended to live. That is our ultimate longing isn't it, not to only have blessing here and now, but eternal blessedness? Our deepest longing is to return to the tree of life, to be with God in the garden and feast on all that He intended for us. He is waiting for us and He will fulfill our longings as we admit our total dependence upon His mercy, love, forgiveness, grace and redemption.

Change
to become different[4]

> *Search me, O God, and know my heart;*
> *test me and know my anxious thoughts.*
> *See if there is any offensive way in me,*
> *and lead me in the way everlasting.*
> *Psalm 139:23-24*

Change, not that stuff in the bottom of my purse; no, the stuff of this mortal life. Things change. People change. Times and seasons change. As summer draws to a close I wane for a bit, until the first cold snap and the fall colors burst on the scene. The changing of seasons is bittersweet.

I was born in the summer, thus that is where my life began and where I long for it to remain, but alas each year summer ends. My entrance into Kindergarten eased this loss and thus my seasonal cycle began to revolve around the school calendar. Going to school for me was an adventure and a joy. I loved my Kindergarten teacher. She was tall, slim and very friendly. Our room was equipped with wooden blocks, puzzles, picture books and a painting easel in the art corner. I remember making paper lollipops, two circles of paper pasted together on a Popsicle stick, color coded and labeled to learn my colors.

I began to love school so much that I would set up a schoolroom in our basement to "teach" the neighbors at the beginning of summer break. We would play school, then after a few days we would be drawn to the surrounding woods to explore or else to cool off in our pool. In the pool we hosted underwater tea parties, held diving contests and choreographed our own water ballet routines. At the end of summer, Mom would take us to garage sales and Kmart to buy clothes for the new school year.

As this school year approaches I am trying to soak in the last days of summer, and prepare for the beginning of a new school year. This year seems significant, not only because I turned forty, or because this summer has been marked with the loss of my Dad, but because of a sense that "the winds are changing". That saying captures how I am feeling as the boys return to school in a week or so. For a time, after my high school graduation and before kids, the school year calendar was replaced; I was a regular calendar follower. When my oldest son began school I was elated to be back on the school year schedule. The past eleven years or so I have been in my element. This year has caused me to grieve as our school-centered days are coming to an end in the near future. No more school supply lists, no more pushing a cart through the aisles piled with new notebooks, pencils, lunchboxes and the myriad accessories for going back to school. This is a real loss for me, so bear with me while I indulge in a little time to mourn.

All of this brings up the heart wrenching question of what will I do with me when the boys "grow up". Last month, my husband and I met with a dear couple on the east coast to ponder this very question. We returned home with an idea of what significance would look like for each of us over the next five years, both individually and as a couple. One interesting "evaluation instrument" we looked at while there was called a change style indicator. It helps you to see how you respond to or navigate change. I know this will not be a surprise, but my husband and I approach change from opposite ends of the spectrum. We actually think differently, and our relational needs are not alike. All of these revelations were very sobering. We discovered there is space between us, yet God in His grace has showed us ways to bridge the gap through communication and love. Although these discoveries were not news to us, I think we both came home in awe, and really humbled that we have this giftedness between us to share with each other, as well as those around us.

My change approach is more intuitive. I long for change, and become restless after a time. This was eye-opening and reassuring at the same time, because I kept thinking something was wrong with me. I often need new direction or new approaches to the same thing or something altogether new to keep me lively. Staying focused on one topic for a very long time saps my energy and creativity. I now see how this can bring variety and joy, not only to me, but to others as well. Seeing that my husband isn't as likely to make changes at a drop of a hat, I can learn to work with this and wait for him, which will enable him to take the time that he needs to prepare for change without me chaffing because he isn't ready.

Change is to be expected and sometimes desired. Change can be dauntingly painful and mysteriously joyous at the same time. I am learning that I can't fight it or run away from it. I want to see the seasonal changes and life changes as friend more than foe. Where is God in all this? He is the author of the seasons. He knows what will open our heart and draw us in. I find that He is right here walking with me through each season, ordaining my days, not surprised or frightened by anything I may face (Psalm 139:16).

Look at me
Look in me
Is there any offensiveness in me?
A way that hurts
A way that causes pain
A way that leads me off
A way that loves
A way that heals
A way that worships You
Lead me in a way that leads to You always
(KSR)

Choose
to select freely and after consideration[5]

This day I call heaven and earth as witnesses against you that I have set before you life and death, blessings and curses. Now choose life, so that you and your children may live and that you may love the LORD your God, listen to his voice, and hold fast to him. For the LORD is your life…
Deuteronomy 30:19-20a

As I look back over the last week or so, I have been the opposite of calm and composed. I have been irritable. I have been tired, cranky, and agitated about many things. I finished my classes at the community college and was looking forward to a less structured schedule, as well as more time to write. Wouldn't you know just when I had more time on my hands; I come down with a case of writer's block. I had been searching my heart, practicing the disciplines of reading the Word, journaling and praying, yet my mind felt lethargic. Nothing seemed to be coming together.

No defining moments. I had looked up several words in the dictionary, and even that favorite adventure was leaving me uninspired. I looked up some words on writing, as I prepared to share with a small group of women about my writing journey. The word that stood out was, compose. Not only was it defined as the act of writing music or literature, but also was related to the concept of calming oneself. Compose yourself, you might say, or "get a grip" is another way of saying it. Just the message I needed.

On Mother's Day, a tender day as my sons and husband affirmed me with touching cards, flowers and a nice breakfast; I thought I was coming out the doldrums. But sometime between the happy morning and returning home from church, my mood had soured.

Later in the afternoon I had settled down. As planned I went to see *Spiderman 3* with my mom and the boys. It was an intense movie with many battles being fought. Near the end of the movie, Peter Parker summarized that while everyone faces internal battles, we always have a choice. His conclusion struck at my heart. All afternoon I had been choosing to give into self-pity, instead of confronting my feelings and working through the issues with God.

I struggled to engage, and was frustrated because I seemingly had nothing to write, yet God came through. During prayer times He reminded me with Scripture about his everlasting nature (Deuteronomy 33:27) and his characteristic offer of being my Helper (Isaiah 41:10). He sent many friends to spend time with me. One friend told me, "Choosing joy is just as much a discipline as other spiritual practices."

It is amazing when I choose to move toward the God of joy, even when I don't feel like it, that the moodiness and the discontent melt away.✺

Clarity
the quality or state of being clear[6]

Send forth your light and your truth, let them guide me;
let them bring me to your holy mountain,
to the place where you dwell.
Psalm 43:3

The word clarity recently piqued my interest, when a friend had asked his prayer team to pray for clarity from God in a new ministry position he had accepted. This was a word that I wanted to know more about. How many of us long for life to be clear? I want my life to be described by words like bright, unclouded and unencumbered by debt, don't you? And I want things to be obvious.

I am often uncertain of what I am doing and if it really matters. Jesus has set me free, why is it that I still live under this fog of uncertainty? Or why does life feel restricted? Many reasons may surface, but one that makes sense to me relates to the amount of truth I am taking in, believing on and acting upon. The opposite can be true as well: How many lies am I listening to? How are these lies influencing my life? I have to be reminded how important it is to be drenched in the word of God. To memorize it, to pray over it and to speak it out loud in praise, these activities bring clarity.

My friend, who asked for clarity, mentioned that he had been struggling with a heaviness of heart and mental clutter. His comment made me think of a popular cleaning coach, called Flylady, who advises housekeepers to de-clutter. Get rid of the things you do not love. She has a whole process outlined on her website. But the main points are to focus on one area at a time and be willing to toss the things that don't really mean anything to you. If I apply this to my life, I need to seek God and ask him to help me get rid of the things in my life that are not pleasing to Him, and that are hindering my ability to love Him and others. This is hard because some of the things I need to get rid of I kind of love. But these things are clouding my perspective.

This summer I returned to places that were haunts of my childhood. It was wonderful to see relatives and catch up. A lot of our time was spent reminiscing about our childhood years or discovering some interesting stories about my grandmother's parents and grandparents. While walking down memory lane, some not so happy memories returned as well. Clutter from the past. This kind of clutter can be very overwhelming.

Thankfully, God had another trip down memory lane planned for me when I got back from these trips. Over the last several months I have been going through the study, *Believing God,* offered by Beth Moore. I had not picked it up in awhile, but thought I would try to finish it up. In God's perfect timing the lesson I had left off on correlated to my journey into the past. On this trip though, I was to focus more on where and when I remembered God's presence and intervention and love in the midst of my journey. It was very clear, that indeed, He was always there, even during the times I believed He forgot about me.

Over the years, shame has been a constant companion. Because of my own sin or the atmosphere in which I grew up, I secretly clung to this companion. Through the lecture that goes along with the lesson, my eyes were opened. God freed me from much confusion, which I had experienced regarding shame. A cloak of shame, that burdened me down in despair. In the lecture, Beth explained that we all have these cloaks; they just have different descriptions embroidered on them. When we became believers, we missed a point about what Jesus had done for us. We thought we needed to hide the shame. Turning the cloak inside out, believing that now the shame has been dealt with, instead we find it turned inward and are held captive by it. We convinced ourselves falsely that we have to wear the shame; it isn't enough for Jesus to take it on for us. This is so revolutionary to me. I knew that I was struggling with something, but it wasn't obvious. I needed someone else to make it clear to me.

Praise be to our God who has freed us, and even when we have allowed ourselves to get into a cycle of defeat, He triumphantly leads us out.᷾

Cram
to pack tight; jam[7]

Praise be to the God and Father of our Lord Jesus Christ, the Father of compassion and the God of all comfort, who comforts us in all our troubles, so that we can comfort those in any trouble with the comfort we ourselves have received from God.
2 Corinthians 1:3-4

I was preparing for a house guest and decided the morning before her arrival that I needed to wash one of our comforters for her bed. As I was cramming the fluffy white thing into my washer, I thought to myself, this is not a good idea; I really should take this to the Laundromat. But since I didn't have time to go, I continued to cram it into the cavity of my less than optimal capacity washer. Later I came back to check on its progress. The clothing piled on the floor waiting for its turn to be washed was squishy and wet. While the washer filled with water, the too tightly crammed comforter allowed water to splash and run out all over the dirty clothes. Ever optimistic, I plunged forward and tried to wrestle the comforter out of the washer into the dryer. I assured myself that the comforter had spun out well enough, but then I noticed some grime from the washer rim on the corner of the comforter. I tried to rub it off and only made it worse. I surrendered and hauled the comforter into a basket and on to the Laundromat.

I brought a book along to read while I waited. The chapter in the book was about "reframing your problems" from God's perspective. The title of the book was *In a Pit with a Lion on a Snowy Day*. That inspired the following entry in my journal: *In a Laundromat with a Comforter on a Humid Day*. This little adversity with the comforter afforded me some time to reflect not only on my laundry dilemma, but also the current state of my life. To put it lightly my life was tightly packed with way too many activities and commitments. I cringed when I opened my planner. I cried out to the Master Scheduler of my days, "Help!" And he rescued me time and time again.

Even when I neglected to create time and space for Him, he optimized my foolish ways and redirected me to His perfect ways. So I met with God in the Laundromat. He reminded me of my growing up years and my embarrassment of having to use a Laundromat. And yet it was a refuge of sorts. We would load up the station wagon, haul in the clothes and visit while we waited. We gave my younger sister rides in the roller carts, and I learned how my step-brother liked his jeans dried so they came out with less wrinkles. As an adult I have often found quiet moments on vacation while doing laundry. And I used to take the boys to Suds N' Duds between camp and vacation to get all the clothes washed at once. We'd buy donut holes and wash them down with soda while we waited. Waiting is good. It gives you time to reflect. And even though I had to pay $4.00 and spend 40 minutes out of my day, the time reading and reflecting was worth it. I even got to play the pinball machine. So the lesson for the day was: Do not cram the comforter into your home washing machine; go to the Laundromat, and enjoy some time with the Comforter of Souls. And a side note: Be careful of how much you are jamming into your life; always ask the Master Scheduler in advance what He wants on the agenda of your day or week.

Cure
to restore to health, soundness, or normality[8]

Praise the LORD.
How good it is to sing praises to our God,
how pleasant and fitting to praise him! He heals the
brokenhearted and binds up their wounds.
Psalm 147:1, 3

Have you ever sought healing from Jesus for yourself or others? Have you been disappointed? I have read several of the gospel accounts over and over, wondering how it could be that so many experienced healing at the moment they sought it. For several years now I have been struggling with a chronic physical problem that has not responded to the prescribed treatments. I was so frustrated one day, I cried out to God, "Please heal me. I know that you are able. Is it my faith that keeps me from complete healing? Why are you not healing me in this?" And ever so quietly, I sensed the invitation to ask for "complete healing." I thought about it, and realized that I did need more than just physical relief from pain; I needed the complete healing of my heart and spirit. I responded by asking in faith for the complete healing. That's when the journey began.

I wish I could report that I have been completely healed. I haven't been, but I have discovered that healing is a process. While I have been to counseling for soul issues and continue to consult doctors for physical ailments, I need to pray and ask God to heal me. I am thankful for the progress in my health and the comfort in my heart as I have groaned, "Your grace is sufficient" (2 Corinthians 12:9).

I have wept over the beauty of the women in the gospels who reached out for Jesus, and were healed. I have mulled over the question Jesus, asked of the invalid, "Do you want to get well?" Wondering if I could answer that question correctly, then would I be healed? But most of all I think that the apparent lack of complete healing has kept me dependent on God. And for that I am truly grateful.

Just the other day, I lamented over this long journey of waiting, still hoping that this set of treatments would be the cure. In the Bible reading for the day I came across the phrase, "for I am the LORD, who heals you" (Exodus 15:26). My heart soared into the reality that over this extended time not only my body, but also my heart had been mending. I observed this in the greater ability to embrace deep joy even in the midst of transitions that used to propel me into despair. God is the One who heals. That is, He is actively, presently and into the future healing each one of us, not just from physical and emotional pain, but from the sting of death, and the wreckage from the fall.~

Define
to determine or identify the essential qualities or meaning of[9]

> *The unfolding of your words gives light;*
> *it gives understanding to the simple.*
> *Psalm 119:130*

I love to look for meaning in everyday occurrences. I have been on a journey these many years seeking answers. I ask why and how come. I wonder to myself. I wonder out loud. I wonder what this life is all about. How did God create this intricate, immense universe that we live in? Why did he let us have words? How did he know that a spoken word could be so healing? Or a story so inviting?

I have been taking three classes, which at first glance seem not to be related. But for me, Intro to Botany, Intro to Acting, and English Comp 102, have a common thread- definition. The dictionary is my favorite book, next to the Bible. I love literature, poems, and even reading my botany text. Sometimes if another student sees me reading the text book they get a bit panicked, because they think they forgot to study for an upcoming exam, but I tell them I'm just reading to help myself better grasp the concepts.

Something else happens in all my classes, not only am I learning the concepts, I see God. I will be listening to a lecture on Critical Thinking, and I realize that the four steps of analysis, synthesis, interpretation, and evaluation are techniques that I have often used to study God's word. And then, I get excited because some of the terms I learn in Literary Analysis give me a springboard to engage with the poetry of the Psalms in a fresh way. Botany is full of the miracles of the atomic world, the design of plants, and the amazing symbiotic relationship God created between humans and plants. Acting class has taken me out of my comfort zone, and I have learned that inhibitions can be an obstacle to relating one's character authentically. Inhibitions may have a negative connotation for some people, but when I looked up its definition, I was interested to see that it would do me well to give up some of mine, especially the ones that keep me from honestly expressing myself, as well as just relaxing in God's sovereignty a bit more often.

These may not seem like gigantic turning points in my life, yet each one affirms my trust in God's goodness, and a desire for us to see Him in all aspects of our lives. Filled with moments defined by a God glimpse or an infusion of His grace transforms my everyday life.

This happened recently during worship service, as I was contemplating a very hectic schedule. I was singing my heart out to God, while simultaneously bemoaning the fact that I had really overbooked my life for the coming two weeks. Don't ask me how this is possible to do both at the same time; it's just one of those marvels of our God-designed brains. And in that moment, through the gentle whisper of the Spirit, the thought occurred to me, *"Why don't you enjoy each day, instead of just pushing through?"* What a relief washed over me. Those two weeks were full and tiring, but everything fell into place, and some things were rescheduled. The daily pressure was relieved by the convergence of God's grace and my openness to walk through each day with Him as my companion and advisor.

He comes to us in words— the words of a friend, the words of a Botany lecture or the words of an English professor sharing his paradigm on thinking. Yet, my favorite place to feast on words is in the Scripture— a psalm that expresses my emotions, a proverb that points out a practical truth and a prophet who was a man just like you and me (James 5:17-18). Defining moments, where the word of God and our minds, hearts and souls connect in the quickening of life, which result in ordinary me understanding something like the metaphor of a wellspring of life, a watering place that never runs dry. May you enjoy his Presence in the coming days. And keep your heart open for His defining moments.

Deliver
to set free[10]

> *The LORD is my rock, my fortress and my deliverer; my*
> *God is my rock, in whom I take refuge. He is my shield*
> *and the horn of my salvation, my stronghold.*
> *Psalm 18:2*

Deliverance is the Lord's business. I was revisiting the story of Moses and the Israelites recently. The Israelites were in captivity under the king of Eygpt. Their cries for deliverance had been heard by God. In the meantime, Moses had fled Egypt, started a family, and took a job tending his father-in-law's flocks. One day Moses was out tending the flocks when he noticed a curious bush. It was on fire, yet the flames were not consuming the bush. Moses moved closer to investigate (Exodus 3:4-6). The LORD saw that Moses was interested, he had Moses' attention; and then God called him by name.

When something unusual happens in our life, do we stop long enough to investigate? Would we be available and able to hear God call our name? How many holy encounters have we missed because we lacked curiosity?

Now that God had Moses' attention, He comes to the point of His visit. (Exodus 3:7-10) God has an assignment for Moses. We can almost see Moses shudder with dread. Not Egypt, anywhere, but there. Remember he had tried once before to deliver the Hebrews, by taking a stand and killing one of the slave drivers. That didn't go very well. Moses had fled for his life from Pharaoh, who hadn't been pleased with Moses' action. Moses' reply tells all: "But Moses said to God, 'Who am I, that I should go to Pharaoh and bring the Israelites out of Egypt?'" (Exodus 3:11). God promises to be with him, but Moses still has some concerns. He begins to think of several reasons why this wouldn't work. He thinks, "I can't stand up to Pharaoh, he'll kill me, and the Israelites don't want to follow me." He asks God who am I to say who you are? What if they don't believe me? And besides I'm not a very eloquent speaker. God answers each of the reasons. He states, "I AM WHO I AM." He enables Moses to perform signs to convince them. He basically says, "We'll get Aaron to speak for you." God reassures Moses that this plan will work. Then God reveals another interesting twist to Moses' mission (Exodus 3:18-20). God foreshadows that this mission is doable, but it will not be simple. Little does Moses know that it will take ten devastating plagues to convince Pharaoh, and it is only a temporary sanction.

Why, we might ask, does deliverance have to be so complicated? God tells Moses why over and over again during the plagues, "By this you will know that I am the LORD…" (Exodus 7:17). God wanted Egypt to know that He is the LORD. He wanted Moses and Aaron to know without a shadow of doubt that God would be their deliverer. And He would prove it to the Israelites.

Here an interesting characteristic of a people in bondage can be noted. Basically they were too discouraged at this point to even begin to hope in deliverance. (Exodus 6:9). All they could think about was their cruel bondage. I have found myself in this situation all too often. But the LORD would not settle for despair. He performed great feats to show Himself all powerful. In the midst of the plagues, God miraculously kept some of the plagues away from the Israelites, showing them that He can overcome their powerlessness.

In this journey of Moses and the Israelites some parallels to my own struggles surfaced. How often I have felt enslaved to a captor. Over the years this captor has worn many masks- Sin, Resentment, Disappointment, Depression and Selfishness- the list is endless.

When Moses reluctantly went to "deliver the captives," he may have thought he would approach Pharaoh, make his request to let them go, and that would be that. But God orchestrated circumstances to show Moses that He alone set the captives free.

Maybe you have someone in your life, like I have that has been difficult to forgive or has caused great discouragement in your life. Maybe like me, you ask why it couldn't have been different. Why was this person allowed to harm me? Why won't they change? We may even go to this person and it seems their heart is hardened toward us over and over. When will I finally realize that this person is not the one who is even able to deliver me? God is my DELIVERER! ⚜

Ending
something that constitutes an end; conclusion[11]

*I am the Alpha and the Omega, the First and the Last,
the Beginning and the End.
Revelation 22:13*

Winter had ended, so the calendar reported. In this moment the realization came over me that I do not handle endings well. Either I bemoan the end of a season or I chafe wondering when it will be over. At times I have looked forward to endings, but often I have found myself at a loss as to my next beginning.

This time of year many churches review the end of Jesus' life on earth. I was revisiting that journey to the cross, and my heart broke as my Savior goes the hard way. And my heart chided me because I was too weak and unwilling to follow Him in His suffering. I desired the easy road. Yet Jesus went all the way. He found the victory. He overcame death. He rose again.

I came across this statement about God's endings in Scripture, "The end of a matter is better than its beginning…" (Ecclesiastes 7:8). God promises us a better ending. When I get bogged down in life's muck and mire, the main thing that pulls me out is the hope of a better life beyond this one. Yet I am in a dilemma because I must still live this life out to its end. I wish we could fast forward to the end of this age and begin the everlasting life, the new life forever. This desire causes a great tension in me. Sometimes I experience this life and agree with Solomon's refrain "All is meaningless." Winter is boring. Loving is hard. Forgive someone, I'd rather die. Ugh!!!! When will this struggle end? I'm waiting for the joy. Where is it?

Then, I hear a quiet whisper of an invitation and reassurance. Jesus knows I need to hear it over and over again. He beckons us to arise, to come with Him (Song of Solomon 2:10-14). He hasn't forgotten us. He wants to hear our voice. He sees us as lovely. Flowers are appearing on the earth and the season of singing has come.

In the meantime, I need to stay by my suffering Savior's side and see Him all the way to the cross and remember His death as He asked us to do. I need His help to die to myself so that His life can overcome mine and make all things new and beautiful in His time (Ecclesiastes 3:11-14).

Another one of my problems with endings has to do with the past. The past has ended in real time, yet it invades my thoughts and causes me to question and doubt. What to do about the past? Is it friend or foe? Has it ended? I think the past will visit me and cause me to question until the day I die.

There are parts of my past that I've never grieved over. This is something that I resist. Grieving is messy. It hurts. Sometimes it causes me to be really angry. Other times it's difficult to stop crying. Yet two familiar scriptural quotes keep coming to mind: "Weeping lasts for the night, but joy comes in the morning" and "Blessed are those who mourn, for they shall be comforted." Weeping and mourning must come first. Joy and Comfort follow in time.

It would be easier if the chorus from the *Joy of the Lord is My Strength* that goes, "If you want joy, you must clap for it" were true. We might be better served if the chorus was "If you want joy, you must mourn for it." But alas, that isn't very cheery is it?

One last bit of challenge concerning the past. Although I think we are to grieve over it, I also see God reminding us not to dwell on it. He has new, fresh beginnings in store for us. Let us continue our journey, and seek Him who is our ultimate joy, comfort and strength in this life and beyond.܀

Epiphany

a usually sudden manifestation or perception of; the essential nature or meaning of something[12]

No temptation has seized you except what is common to man. And God is faithful; he will not let you be tempted beyond what you can bear. But when you are tempted, he will also provide a way out so that you can stand up under it. Therefore, my dear friends, flee from idolatry.
1 Corinthians 10:13-14

I have a confession to make. I have been looking for Christmas under the tree for many years now. This tendency manifests itself in my actions. I host Christmas parties, decorate the whole house, bake cookies, buy and wrap presents with care. All of this is very satisfying to me because I love Christmas; yet something is missing. I set up our Advent candles, meditate on Christmas devotions and sing the carols with heartfelt joy. But the joy fades soon after the tree is packed up and only cookie crumbs and candy canes remain.

Last year something new happened. I experienced the peace of the season. Peace accompanied me, not busyness and tiredness, my perennial companions of the holidays. And no complaining, "Oh, I can't wait until this is over." Or even worse, "What will I do with myself during the bleak winter ahead?" I still engaged in many of the holiday trimmings, and yet I did do some things differently. I didn't put all of my hope into a magical Christmas season. I didn't demand that Christmas come through for me. I didn't try to recapture some childhood ideal. I just enjoyed it. I let it be the Christmas that it was going to be. I didn't get upset if it wasn't exactly like years past. And most of all I focused my heart on the true meaning of Christmas, Christ's arrival into our world to save mankind from our sins (Matthew 1:21).

One December morning, my agenda included gathering my family around to decorate the tree while listening to carols, but alas no one was to be found. My husband had graciously retrieved the decorations from the attic, put up the tree lights, and had then retreated to his newspaper. I asked the boys if they wanted to help decorate the tree. "Not really," was their reply. So I sat in the corner to cry. I won't go through all my pining, but my pity party included the realization that no one would care if the tree was up and decorated, except me. I had to decide to put it up for my own joy. It was hard, but I'm glad I did. And really I think the three guys in my life would have wondered where it was, if I had given in to my "nobody cares" mood.

When I look back on why last year was different, the event of putting up the Christmas tree became an epiphany of sorts, a moment that revealed the demands of my heart. Since I believe the Holy Spirit resides in my life through faith in Christ, I will give Him all the credit for changing my experience. He pointed out to me that I have idolized the holiday for far too long.

Thus began my turning away from Christmas idolatry. For the most part our Christmas may not have looked much different than years past, but it definitely was experienced with less stress and greater joy. My demands were transformed into desire to spend more time with friends and family, as well as time to just be quiet. Instead of the flurry of the season, I sensed God inviting me to get to know Him better. Christmas had come to reside in my heart.

Expect

to anticipate or look forward to the coming or occurrence of[13]

The LORD is good to those whose hope is in him,
to the one who seeks him;
it is good to wait quietly
for the salvation of the LORD.
Lamentations 3:25-26

Expectations run high around the Christmas holiday. We each have a belief that something will happen. Some may hope for special moments with family; others may be looking forward to getting the coolest new gaming unit. Over the years I have had various expectations, sometimes they are met and other times I have been disappointed.

I was surprised recently as I walked into one of our department stores and the logo for the holiday read, "Love transforms everything". I thought of Jesus, and considered this, "His love transforms everything". The store, of course, wants us to create an atmosphere that includes beautiful decorations and wrappings bought from their store, as well as all the gifts we hope will make our loved ones pleased for the day. Gifts are pleasant, and we all love to give and receive them. But the promise of the department store will only last for a season. God's gifts are everlasting. The gift of His Son can truly transform lives. His promises can make our hearts leap for joy.

The book of Isaiah, which is both prophetic and poetic, has a psalm tucked into chapter twelve. The third verse fills my heart with hope: "With joy you will draw water from the wells of salvation" (Isaiah 12:3). Salvation is God's ultimate Christmas present. And its joys are to be drawn upon as one would daily draw water from a well. Maybe your joy has run dry. Maybe your motto is different. Something like: "Sin ruins everything" or "Love disappoints." Our present life is tainted by death and despair, yet there is more.

I have often heard myself or others desperately cry, "Restore the joy of MY salvation." A closer look at the actual verse may astound us. It actually states, "Restore to me the joy of YOUR salvation…" (Psalm 51:12a). Salvation is what God has provided for us. He is the one who can remind us of its deep joy in the face of our various trials and heartaches.

As you eagerly await the hopes and joys of Christmas, may the Lord Jesus, Himself, encourage you with these words from Scriptures regarding a future day.

> . . . so Christ was sacrificed once to take away the sins of many people; and he will appear a second time, not to bear sin, but to bring salvation to those who are waiting for him. (Hebrews 9:28)

What a comfort to realize the second advent of Jesus is to gather us to Him and the life where sin and sighing flee away.∽

Focus
to concentrate attention or effort [14]

*May he give you the desire of your heart
and make all your plans succeed.
Psalm 20:4*

Every year I evaluate the focus of my life. As I was thinking about specific goals, I was once again drawn to my ever faithful friend, my dictionary. I am quite amazed at the joy and comfort I receive from these defining moments. With God, this tome of words with its definitions takes on deeper meaning.

During a recent dictionary search, I looked up goal, and that led me to ambition, aim, aspiration, and other inspiring words. I jotted them down returning later to see that I had underlined some related synonyms. This brought me to the word focus, and its definition. This raised the question concerning the focus of my interest and activities this coming year. I did some doodling with other words that stood out to me, which included purpose, expect, linger, continue, train, celebrate, and dream. I did not know where all these words were leading me, but the central desire was to develop a deeper relationship with God. I longed for His purpose for my life. I hoped to linger in His presence more often in the coming year. My goal was to continue on the path of prayer, to converse with our holy God, and to seek out His word to train me for life and loving. I expected God to lead me in my pursuit of knowing His heart and encouraging others with words. My aim was to infuse all of these endeavors with an attitude of daily celebration. As the prayer of the psalmist asked, I also asked God to grant this desire of my heart to stay focused on Him. My endeavors will succeed as I submit my plans and motives to Him.

Sometimes my vision gets blurred by all the options this world throws at me. The final outcome of this dictionary search and doodling was a scrapbook page designed as a visual aid. I would look at it to keep me focused on my desire to follow God wholeheartedly.

The visual "definition" of my ambitions will remind me to ask God to keep my mind and heart focused on Him. Two ways to accomplish this is to ask Him to search me (Psalm 139:23-24) and to place my heart under the scrutiny of His word (Hebrews 4:12). My prayer is that you will seek after Him, longing for His focus to clearly lead you on the path of life.⚜

Gospel

the message concerning Christ, the kingdom of God, and salvation[15]

After John was put in prison, Jesus went into Galilee, proclaiming the good news of God. "The time has come," he said. "The kingdom of God is near. Repent and believe the good news!"
Mark 1:14-15

Have you ever been locked out of a place which you needed to get into? During spring break I went to visit with my sisters in New Jersey. And in particular to help my sister who had delivered twins almost two years earlier. She was expecting again, and needed help to reduce her risk of an early delivery.

I went out to run some errands for her, while she and the kids were resting. My plan was to zip in and out of the store, and get back before naptime was over. I was doing really well until I realized at the check out that I couldn't find my keys. I retraced my steps through the store. I checked customer service, and the nice young man at the register suggested that I left them in the car. I went out to the car to discover that not only were the keys in the locked car, but that the car itself was running. It was a rental car that ran so quietly I hadn't noticed that I forgot to turn it off and to take the keys with me.

I called the local police. They assured me that they would come in twenty minutes or so. As I waited by the car, the warm spring morning started churning into a rainy, cold afternoon. I retreated under the awning in front of the store with my full cart. Although calling a locksmith was the next logical step to take, I persisted in waiting for the police.

As I waited I started a conversation with God. "God, why did this happen? How could I be so stupid?" No answer, but a prompting to ask Him to send me a locksmith. There was no reason to not just go and call one, but I sensed that I needed to just ask and see what would happen. So I asked God to send me a locksmith. Even after I asked, I still assured God that I knew He didn't have to send me one, and that I could call one anytime. Yet I waited, giving the police a few more minutes to show up.

Just as I decided to go make my phone call, a truck with yellow lights on top pulled up. The sign on its side door advertised, *Road Runner Roadside Assistance*. I thought it was a special police unit. As he came past me I waved him down. He was not a policeman, but a locksmith from

Illinois! I told him my predicament, and he happily unlocked my car for free. I told him that I had prayed, and he said, "I guess God heard you". I definitely knew that God had heard me.

God was reassuring me that He is faithfully present every moment and for any need. As a child, I had heard the good news that God loved me so much that He gave His one and only Son to be my Savior. My childhood faith assured me that one day I would be with Jesus in heaven. Since that time He has been revealing his love to me in many ways. The good news is not only that we can live with Him forever, but also that we can depend on Him in our everyday life. This situation reminded me how many times over the years that God has reminded me that He will never leave nor forsake me (Hebrews 13:5).

Who doesn't need a little good news now and then? This good news is something we can go back to again and again. Sometimes as Easter approaches, it seems like I'm just rehearsing a nice story, instead of celebrating the greatest event in history. God became man and dwelt among us (John 1:14). He came to give us life and life abundantly (John 10:10). He gave up His life on our behalf and considered it a joy (Hebrews12:2). The amazing scene where the huge boulder has been rolled away from the tomb always makes me want to shout, "Hooray!" That which seemed impossible really happened. Jesus rose from the dead. We are told that we can experience this same power in our lives once we've understood and embraced the sacrifice he made for us (Ephesians 1:18-21).

May the One who sent me a locksmith, send His Holy Spirit to unlock your heart and give you the key to life through the gospel.୶

Home

one's place of residence; a familiar or usual setting[16]

*In my Father's house are many rooms; if it were not so,
I would have told you. I am going there to prepare a place
for you. And if I go and prepare a place for you,
I will come back and take you to be with me
that you also may be where I am.
John 14:2-3*

Home can be a house, habitat or headquarters. It may even be an establishment providing residence and care for people with special needs, like a children's home or a nursing home. Many images arise when we think of home. Many feelings surface as well. Maybe we feel warmth and love, or maybe pain and loneliness. Many people consider home the place where they were born or grew up.

My childhood home was built by my parents when I was two. By the time it suffered a house fire, I was overseas, eighteen, and had not lived there for several years. My father was living there then, but I had left this home when my parents divorced. I was twelve years old at the time, but the memory of that place holds both fondness and pain. It's where I fell in love with the outdoors, building imaginary "homes" in the woods, ice skating on the neighbor's pond, and picking blackberries in August.

We moved to several other houses with my step-father over the years, each one with its own unique qualities. But the first home, the A-Frame on Slusser Road in rural western New York, is the house that comes to mind when I think of home. The other houses never could take its place.

I have resided in other places since leaving New York, but not having a childhood home to return to has left an emotional void in me. One of the most appealing promises of the gospel is that Jesus is presently preparing a place for us. Since my childhood home no longer exists, my hope is now set on that future home.

My husband and I have a wonderful home, recently remodeled with this great porch and a large family room, which gives us much pleasure and sense of home. Yet there are days when my longing for home, an intangible desire, wakens much grief in me. I want to go home. That's when another marvelous promise of the gospel is brought home to my heart. Home *is* where the heart is, or in other words where the heart abides (Luke 12:34; John 15:10).

Are you at home with Jesus? Do you feel relaxed and comfortable with Him, in a holy sense, not a casual one? Does He put you at ease when you enter His presence through prayer? Do you find yourself in familiar surroundings or on familiar ground when you enter His presence through the Scripture? Jesus longs for us to know Him, not just with our heads, but with our hearts. He wants us to be at home with Him and with His love for us. So when you get lonely for home, I hope images of our Savior come to mind. Picture Him waiting to meet with you in your favorite spot at your house. Imagine what He's doing in preparation for your arrival at your heavenly one. And in the meantime remember He is always near; ready to be that place of comfort and home that you long for.

Hope
to cherish a desire with anticipation[17]

*May your unfailing love rest upon us, O Lord,
even as we put our hope in you.
Psalm 33:22*

      A common activity for the New Year is to make resolutions. I don't usually bother with the tradition, but I do like to reflect on the past year. Asking the Lord to help me make adjustments to my schedule, usually results from this type of reflection. I recommit to seeking the Lord daily and continue to pursue His hopes, dreams and desires for my life.

      Usually after the holidays, I get into a winter funk. Over the years I have learned not to fight the slowdown of this season. It is a season to store up energy for the upcoming growing seasons of spring and summer. If you are a winter lover, you're probably going to smile at my recent revelations about this often cold and lonely time of the year. But I began to think about two things. What did I like about winter as a child that could cheer me through the season? And what are some comforts with which I could surround myself now?

One of my favorite childhood activities was ice skating on a pond near our house. To get through the winter I decided to buy ice skates and enjoy the outdoors. Another comfort to get me through the winter included grabbing a hot cocoa with a cozy blanket and curling up in a chair with a good book.

Outdoor activities and creature comforts are wonderful remedies for the winter blues, but what about the hope and joy of the Lord. Hope sometimes eludes me; it is an essential ingredient of my faith. Jesus is my hope. His presence fills me with hope. However, hope is one of those words that could use defining in my life. There is an interesting verse in Proverbs that unveils the importance of hope. It says this, "Hope deferred makes the heart sick, but a longing fulfilled is a tree of life" (Proverbs 13:12). Hope put off or misplaced causes soul anguish. As I sense despair in my life, a possible root cause could be that hope has been snuffed out. This has been very revealing to me and needs more contemplation, but much of my struggle with depressing thoughts is directly related to where my hope is resting, or more importantly, on whom it is resting.

The second half of the verse gives light to what will restore our hope and the joy of life.

Desire is another way to express hope. Desire longs for fulfillment. When we allow God to fulfill us, then our life will be more like it was intended to be. This side of Eden, we are closed off from "the tree of life," yet in this context, I think the writer compares fulfillment of desire to what it would have been like if we had been able to eat from the tree of life. Alas, sin got in the way, producing fear that often overshadows our hope.

Hope gets displaced by fear because deep down I realize that my own self-effort, the comfort of passing pleasures or the temporal love of another person cannot sustain my desire for continuous, complete fulfillment. Only the Creator can satisfy my deepest needs.

When I thirst,
You offer me Drink
When I hunger,
You offer me Satisfaction
When I wander,
You offer me Home
When I stumble,
You offer me Your Hand
When I doubt,
You offer me Hope
(KSR)

Husbandry
the control or judicious use of resources[18]

> *For your Maker is your husband —*
> *the LORD Almighty is his name —*
> *the Holy One of Israel is your Redeemer;*
> *He is called the God of all the earth.*
> *Isaiah 54:5*

"Mary, Mary, quite contrary. How does your garden grow?" So goes the familiar nursery rhyme. Now that winter is past and the birds are singing, my mind wanders to gardening. I can relate to Mary, for some reason I have been quite contrary most of March, and am hoping to shake it as the sun shines again and the warmer weather beckons me to get out in the yard to work in the flower beds. My mother and I reserved a plot at the community garden and plan to dabble in growing some vegetables there.

Many a spiritual lesson has come to me in the garden. As a child my mother kept a garden and her mother had gardened as well. As a teenager my family cultivated vegetables and bought local produce to sell at a roadside stand for our family income. Of course, as a teenager, I grumbled quite a bit about gardening, but now I am drawn to it.

My next question to myself went like this: "Kel, Kel, quite contrary. How grows your spiritual garden?" Lately it has felt barren; the winter debris hasn't been cleared out enough for the spring growth to flourish. Was I willing to allow the Master Gardener do his pruning, planting and nurturing?

One lonely day in March I needed to hear that "my Maker is my husband". I went on a search in my dictionary to see the origins and meaning of the word husband. As often is the case my search yielded some gems, as well as leading me to related words that also encouraged me in my relationship with God.

What is a husband according to Webster's? Master of a house, a married man, a manager or steward. These meanings occur under the noun form. Wives will be interested to note that husband can also be a verb. In this form it means to manage prudently and economically, or to use sparingly.[19] As I contemplated what kind of "husband" God is toward us, I could see Him in these definitions.

He is my Master. He is the master of the house, He promises to inhabit or dwell in those who abide in Him. He is a "married man" in that Christ calls himself the Bridegroom, and the church His bride. And what a faithful husband He is. He is great at managing our lives, even with the little we have to offer.

The word husbandry brings us back to the garden imagery. We can see God as the one who cultivates good things into our lives. He is an expert at judiciously using resources, yet his resources are limitless (Ephesians 3:16; Philippians 4:19).

The word husband has its root in a word related to bower. Not a very familiar word to us, but full of the reasons one may be drawn to a garden. A bower is a place to dwell or inhabit. It can mean "a shelter (as in a garden) made with tree boughs or vines twisted together"[20]. Its definition creates an image of a safe intimate place to go for rest and refreshment. It amazes me that the Almighty LORD desires fellowship with each one of us. He calls us to Himself in order to remind us of His lavish love and unending ability to care for us, as well as to prepare us to serve Him. Many of these thoughts are like a meandering path in the garden. I hope you will take some time to linger in the garden with the Maker.

Plea to the Gardener

Prepare the soil of my barren heart
Pour on the revitalizing compost
Press the light into the dark
Plow under the dead debris
Provide the sunshine and the seed
Plant your life inside of me
Plan the design of my plot
Pluck the weeds of discontent
Prune back the overgrowth
Produce the fruit of yieldedness
(KSR)

Journey

an act or instance of traveling from one place to another; a day's travel[21]

Blessed are those whose strength is in you,
who have set their hearts on pilgrimage.
Psalm 84:5

    I love to travel. Planning our next destination is often the topic of conversation, when my husband and I are returning from a trip. We dream about the possibilities. We discuss the benefits of going to certain places during certain times of the year. While trips are fun and exciting at the time, I often come back from a trip a little blue. I miss the freedom from responsibility. The day after a trip I usually want to sleep or feel a great pressure to get something done.

    We just returned from a great family time at Sunset Bay, New York. Our days included coffee in the morning, meals throughout the day, walks on the beach and watching the sunset each evening. Now that I am home, I am back to figuring out my schedule. What do I need to get done before classes start in three weeks? How can I stick to a "one day at a time" philosophy, when it seems so many duties are facing me? Laundry, grocery shopping, doctor's appointments, catching up with friends and some summer school assignments loom before me.

I'd rather just go back to bed, but the day is calling. We often think of a journey as traveling from place to place, but from its French root, *jour*, there is a sense of daily. It is not easy to live with my longing for a journey to a new place and the reality of routine. My romantic side wants to live in the great hope of the next destination, but my practical side needs to exist in the daily. How can I add a little romance to the daily?

The answer can be realized in the mysterious presence of God. For instance, God's presence with Moses and the Israelites was a daily reality. While they were wandering the wilderness, the presence of God set the agenda for their day. It is interesting to note that the word for journey in Hebrew literally meant to break camp. The Israelites camped out until God initiated the next move. (Numbers 9:15-23). To be attune to God's movement in my life takes paying attention. This takes time, energy and faith. I want to become more and more attuned to his Spirit and to respond with joyful obedience. I don't know how this looks specifically, any more than the Israelites probably knew where they would go next. The main thing they knew was that they wanted God's presence to be in their midst. To be absorbed with God's presence is my ultimate heart's desire. I want to wake up longing for His presence whether I am in a romantic state of mind or a practical state of mind. No matter what life brings my way, I want to be found enjoying His company.⌘

Love
warm attachment, enthusiasm, or devotion[22]

> *Therefore tell the people: This is what the LORD*
> *Almighty says: 'Return to me,' declares the LORD*
> *Almighty, 'and I will return to you,'*
> *says the LORD Almighty.*
> *Zechariah 1:3*

Does anyone really fall in love in the winter? Spring with its bursting song and backdrop of flowers and budding trees seems like a more likely season to fall in love. Summer with its long, warm days beckons us to stay in love, enjoying the pleasures of each others' company. Autumn grants us moments to linger on walks through the fallen leaves holding onto those we love and have loved. Winter drives us indoors, sometimes to the warmth of the hearth and the comfort of snuggling up in our beds, but the cold creeps in and our passions wane. We begin to feel lonely, and to wonder if there will ever again be anything to look forward to besides cold floors, and bleak landscapes.

It is easy to feel stuck in the winter. I don't really want to get up to face another day. I make little routines to propel me forward, but I lack the motivation that I have during the other seasons of the year. Yet love is love the whole year through. The unfailing love of God never changes. His love is constant. He doesn't need a special holiday like Valentine's to demonstrate His love. He has already sent His love. (Romans 5:8) And if God did send us a Valentine's card or those little candy hearts with messages on them I think they would say something like "Return to Me."

While studying the Minor Prophets this winter, I have noticed a love theme. Although their messages are filled with a lot of blood and gore mixed with haunting odes of judgment, their underlying tone resonates with the yearning of a lover. Our Creator God, who desires to pour out compassion, rather than wrath, calls out through the prophets, "Seek me and live" (Amos 5:4). He is a loving father who will do everything necessary to rid his children of their foolish beliefs and practices that only bring them sorrow (Psalm 16:4).

It is so overwhelming to realize that the God who created all the seasons pursues my heart. He is so committed to my well-being that He allows these winters of my soul. I may never fall in love with winter itself, but my heart does thrill at the One who loves me so; the One who never leaves me to wallow in my puddle of self-pity. He loves us so incredibly much; I can't even express it. Not even candy heart messages will do.❦

New

beginning as the resumption or repetition of a previous act or thing; made or become fresh[23]

I will give you a new heart and put a new spirit in you;
I will remove from you your heart of stone
and give you a heart of flesh.
Ezekiel 36:26

Fresh starts, that's what I love about a new year. Today the house was emptied of the noisy companionship of our two teenage boys. I miss them, yet I must confess that ever since the boys have been in school all day, I have come to cherish the hush that comes over the house when they are gone. After I got out of bed, I got right into "undecorating" the house from Christmas. I even took the tree and lights down, a job usually delegated to my husband. I guess I was sort of saying good-bye to that tree. I decided to go for the pre-lit, mostly assembled tree at the after Christmas sale. Although my youngest son did ask that I keep the old one for him to use someday.

I think I'm in the melancholy mode lately in regards to the boys growing up. The oldest has three semesters left in his high school career; I can't even type without tears welling up. As my emotions ride the waves of changing times, I am thankful for the constancy of God's love and grace in our lives.

As the New Year unfolds, I am wakened by God to continue the pursuit of passing along encouraging words, as He encourages me. So, although this time a tight theme isn't coming together, I wanted to share some of the journey I've been on the last few weeks, as I've sat with the Lord Jesus remembering both His nativity and Kingship.

After Christmas I start thinking about the next year. Once the holiday hubbub calms down, I take my annual trek to buy a calendar refill for my appointment notebook. This time I also bought "to-do" list filler pages because a new year brings many opportunities to get things done; and of course, I want to keep track of them all.

I started musing about who started the whole idea of a "to-do" list. This led me back to the age old question of "being" pitted against "doing". I am not saying there is not a time and place for the "to-do" list, or even that such an activity is less holy than stillness, yet being still is vital to our enjoyment of the doing. So here is my proposition to myself and to you as well: "Why not start making out a "to-be" list before the "to-do" list?"

Here is an example:

Things "To-Be" Today
Kind
Patient
Willing to Listen
Friendly

These are attributes that reflect "Christ in us". They won't be as hard to accomplish, if we ask Him to release them into our lives each day. Then meeting the demands of our "to-do" lists may be easier as well. New priorities may emerge as well.✺

Persevere

to persist in a state, enterprise, or undertaking in spite of counterinfluences, opposition, or discouragement [24]

Perseverance must finish its work so that you may be mature and complete, not lacking anything.
James 1:4

Have you ever noticed that your whole body shudders when you hear the word perseverance? It sounds like torture, and no wonder since it has the word "severe" in it. How will I make it through the difficult work of daily living? I chide myself "You just need to get your priorities right," or "You need balance". These ring true, but I often get discouraged because my definition has more to do with equal shares, than with steadiness and counterbalance.

In *Having a Mary Heart in a Martha World,* Joanna Weaver illustrates balance with a teeter-totter. While it may be fun to adjust each rider's weight to get the teeter-totter balanced, it is just as much fun, as well as energizing to go up and down. This illustration really helped me to see that in life's ebbs and flows there exists a type of balance, which has to do with rhythm.

I love rhythm, even though I have been accused of lacking it musically by my percussionist son. But he is talking about keeping a beat, which I agree I am not good at. I love to move with music, I can't clap along to save my life, but I love the joy that a song produces in my heart and soul.

This teeter-totter rhythm describes my life. I can steadily go up and down in my emotions, back and forth in my interests, in and out with my attempts with relating to God and others. Sometimes joy is pumping out of me like a newly dug oil well, other times I am drawn by degrees back into despair. This happened recently. I was out of synch. I was down, more than up. I was out and about, more than in and listening to the sweet refrains of God's reassuring love. I was looking out for me, rather than reaching out to others.

You might say I was in a "cadenza". This is a musical term that I came across in one of my dictionary adventures. I thought it was a fitting description of my life. A cadenza is a difficult solo passage in a musical work.[25] Have you ever noticed that despair mostly arrives when you are all alone? We may have some solo passages, but God ultimately is working our parts into the overall piece. I'm so glad He doesn't leave us to carry out the whole work by ourselves.

As I was journaling through my despondency, a very humorous, yet touching vignette came out on the page. I'll share my confession and subsequent epiphany:

I have fallen into a pit. I am flat on my face and am trying to pick myself up. I tell myself it's no use- the pit is too deep. My face is covered with mud. It is dark. God whispers in my ear 'It is only night. Sit up. Wipe off your face; open your eyes.' I look around, and I am sitting in the middle of a puddle. I stand up, try to brush away the muck and mire. My God beckons me. He holds out his torch to light the way. He offers me his hand with a smile playing at the corners of his mouth. I let out a giggle, it was only a puddle. We walk along the torch lit path. The full moon rises; dispels the darkness. A warm breeze drapes itself around me like a stole. My Savior in a low voice says, "I love you, so".

He comes to lift us up, and calls us by name. Then he awaits our response (Isaiah 28:23). Perseverance is attending to the loving invitation to deeper life. It is ours through practiced joy in the midst of trials. It is proof of our growing faith. Perseverance is doing its prescribed work, which is to bring us to maturity. So embrace it my friends. We lack nothing with Jesus (Psalm 23:1).

He will give us day by day just what we need. Am I willing to receive it? And from that abundance, am I willing to offer it right back to Him in worship? ⌘

Residue

something that remains after a part is taken, separated, or designated or after the completion of a process[26]

Then I acknowledged my sin to you and did not cover up my iniquity. I said, "I will confess my transgressions to the LORD" — and you forgave the guilt of my sin.
Psalm 32:5

I have always wondered whether I should consider myself a spring cleaning or fall cleaning type of person. To tell you the truth, I am neither. I clean when the spirit moves me, and when I do, it is mostly surface cleaning. I have been known to use cleaning systems, but often fall out of the routines. My present system is to clean what looks most disgusting to me at the moment. Today the kitchen floor was screaming for a good scrubbing, not that I actually scrub any floor in this house, but the kitchen floor had my attention. After I vacuumed the floor, I was thinking about some dirt that had been neglected in the corners and baseboards of the kitchen. Usually I ignore the residue in these areas, but today, I decided to throw a sponge in the mop bucket, get down on my knees to scrub those areas, and then mop the the floor. One thing led to another and I caught myself scrubbing the baseboards, as well as wiping down the lower wall and even the back door. It felt good to scour the dirt and grime away.

As often happens, I started thinking about a spiritual parallel to my mundane task. I wondered how much sin residue gets overlooked in the corners of my heart. Just as I don't really have scheduled appointments with my floor or deep cleaning ventures, most of my heart cleansing comes when my heart can't cope with the sin anymore. I confess the obvious, like regular mopping where I clean up the most visible dirt. I know some sin is left unconfessed, yet I ignore it, like the residue in the corners of my kitchen. Then one day the sin depresses me so much, I have to pay attention to it. The accumulated sin seems more difficult to overcome; I find that the only way to confess it is to get on my knees.

An insidious sin that I often overlook is pride. Believing that I can live life in my own strength is my downfall. To overcome this I must humble myself, and literally getting on my knees can help my perspective, but really it is the choice to surrender that leads to a release from pride's strong hold on my heart (James 4:10; 1 Peter 5:6). In the recesses of my heart are tendencies to sin that I am learning may have roots in my heredity. This type of sin is harder to overcome because it is easy to excuse as part of my personality. I have been exploring these strongholds in order to be freed from their influence. As I am aware of their hold on me I can recognize them, and ask God to help me resist the temptation they represent in my life. The enemy takes every opportunity to lure me into these tendencies, so as to render me ineffective for God's work.

Two things that have been hounding me lately have been tiredness and discouragement. I think the tiredness comes from fighting the discouragement. I spent a lot of time trying to figure out what was wrong with me. I was eating and exercising. I was spending time in God's word and praying, but I was weighed down. A friend suggested that perhaps the enemy was purposefully tempting me to be discouraged. This perspective freed me to cry out to God for release. The discouragement lifted. Now when discouraging thoughts start, I ask, "Wait a minute, where is this coming from?" Then the Holy Spirit helps me overcome the temptation to despair.

While our enemy is looking for opportune times to trap us, our Heavenly Father is offering us opportunities to become more holy. Recognizing the residue of sin in my heart and then confessing are kindnesses from God that bring about a cleansed and refreshed heart.

Resist
to exert oneself so as to counteract or defeat[27]

*It is for freedom that Christ has set us free.
Stand firm, then, and do not let yourselves
be burdened again by a yoke of slavery.
Galatians 5:1*

The courage to resist sin comes to us in the proportion that we submit to and remember God is the only one who can deliver us. We need reminders. We need the truth before us at all times. One major strategy of our enemy is to lie and distort our belief about God and ourselves. Freedom from oppression comes through resisting the lies and replacing them with dependence upon the Truth. I think that warfare analogies can be helpful as we strive to live in freedom, but we should not look to this as the only analogy for the Christian walk. So as I try to articulate some truths God has been putting upon my heart regarding warfare and resistance, I want to keep our focus on the truth that Jesus is the Victor and the Warrior who came to destroy the works of the devil. He has provided us with strategies to protect ourselves until He returns for the final victory.

God has given us His Word and prayer to combat the lies and schemes of the devil. Comparing three key passages, James 4:4-7, 1 Peter 5:6-11, and Ephesians 6:10-18, we find directives for how to engage in combat against the evil one. As I meditated on these Scriptures, I noticed some new "weapons" that I hadn't designated as such before.

I see a couple strategies. First, guard against becoming friends with the world. Secondly, since God desires full devotion and offers grace, submit to Him. Give in to His ways, as this leads to freedom and a desire to resist the devil. Resisting the enemy is a defensive stance, while submitting oneself to God empowers us. Submission to God appears to be a prerequisite for the ability to resist or stand firm, as well as exercising self-control and alertness.

When speaking of spiritual warfare, Paul exhorts us to "stand firm." This raises the question, "What does resistance or standing firm look like?" This passage in Ephesians 6, like the others, starts out with a plea to rely upon the Lord God. First, by James we are told to submit to God, then Peter encourages us to humble ourselves to God, and finally, Paul says to be strong in the Lord. Our success in resisting the devil is completely wrapped up in our reliance upon the Lord God Almighty. When one faces a formidable enemy, courage is strengthened by the knowledge that one has an experienced Commander who has great resources at hand.

The best way to resist the enemy is to rest in the truth that the LORD will fight for you (Exodus 14:13-14, Deuteronomy 3:22). God's strategy for warfare hasn't changed. Even the Israelites were commanded to stand firm. In our active lives it is very hard to be still and wait for God's deliverance. I have often missed seeing God's glory and experiencing His divine intervention because I fight in my own strength and rely on my own wisdom. When I worry and plot how to overcome adversity in my life, all I get is more stress. But when I rest in Him, then I am still enough to see His hand at work.

Resting in God does not mean that we sit in complete inactivity. But it can mean soaking in His Word, learning how to pray effectively, and following His lead in our lives. Often this takes a literal sitting still to read, concentrate and listen to the Holy Spirit through the Scripture.

Recently I decided to pick up the neglected discipline of committing Scripture to memory. I took some verses that I wrote on note cards and headed out for a walk. I was able to memorize the first few verses of Psalm 27 by the end of my walk.

My husband was out of town having left that same morning. I was a bit discouraged because I was dreading his absence. Two weeks without him home to back me up with the boys or to just talk in person over the daily struggles of life seemed like an unfair trial. The first night he was gone I lost my temper with the boys.

Two or three days into the week I took the van in for some work. On that same day I heard that our friend's father passed away. On the heels of that news, the car place called to inform me that the van needed some brake work; and really bad news, the transmission needed to be replaced. Now what? I called my husband and cried because I didn't want to deal with second opinions on the van. I just didn't want to handle this problem by myself. After I got off the phone, I prayed, "God, I forgot to ask you to help me with the van, please deal with it for me."

Then the verse I memorized earlier that week popped into my mind (that's the benefit of the discipline). The verse was this one "…though war break out against me, even then, I will be confident." (Psalm 27:3). I replied in my heart, "Yes, Lord, I will be confident in You. You are my light and my salvation, whom shall I fear? You are the stronghold of my life, of whom shall I be afraid?"(Psalm 27:1). Not even twenty minutes later the dealer called me back. In reviewing our records the transmission was under warranty. Hallelujah! God fought for me! And He fights for each of us daily.⌇

Retreat
a place of privacy or safety[28]

> *My soul thirsts for God, for the living God.*
> *When can I go and meet with God?*
> *Psalm 42:2*

The squeal and swoosh of the school bus brakes have returned to the neighborhood. Just when I was getting into a summer routine, the bell rings for classes to start. I am ready to finish my final semester at UM-St. Louis. I am one of those non-traditional students, who late in life decided she wanted her college education after all. As I gather notebooks and textbooks into my backpack, I begin to lament that my unhurried times in the gazebo gazing off into the cosmos of God's heart will soon be over.

Instead, my time will be filled with huge amounts of reading and writing papers, as well as collaborating with other students on projects to fulfill our requirements. How will I meet with God in the midst of this chaotic pace? It occurs to me that I will have to plan "retreats" during the week. This will take discipline because some days I will be overwhelmed and others just apathetic about anything. These feelings occur on a regular basis, so I want to plan in advance a strategy to ward off complacency.

Thankfully most of my classes start late morning this semester, giving me more time to linger in the refuge of the porch swing or snatched moments of contemplation in the gazebo. This all sounds a bit romantic, but sometimes I need to view my life in these terms to find the adventure and joy of it all.

I like the concept of a retreat because it offers an intentional way to escape the pressures of life. Usually a retreat takes place at a certain time and location with a group of people to reflect on God. Since I don't really have time for one of those right now, I want to incorporate the idea of retreat into my regular schedule. I want to set aside time to enjoy God's presence in the daily chaos of life.

In reading Emilie Griffin's, *Wilderness Time*, a book about spiritual retreats, my interest increased in designing personal retreats for other weary travelers in the midst of ordinary life. I don't know where this interest will lead me, but I hope to see some fruit in my personal life and hopefully extend an invitation in the future for others to design their own personal retreats.

In the meantime, may I encourage you to spend some time thinking about and asking yourself, "When can I meet with God?" And maybe even contemplate why this is a good idea.~

Root
an underlying support; the essential core[29]

> *So then, just as you received Christ Jesus as Lord,*
> *continue to live in him, rooted and built up in him,*
> *strengthened in the faith as you were taught, and*
> *overflowing with thankfulness.*
> *Colossians 2:6-7*

In a botanical sense, a root is that structure of the plant that usually grows below ground. In its most basic function the root system absorbs water and stores food for the plant, as well as providing support. Roots are very adaptable. Roots grow above ground with runners to sustain growth and fruitfulness, as in strawberry patches. Roots provide food, like potatoes. Roots are adaptable, growing in soil, in water, and even in the air. Some grow deep and spread wide. Some grow just beneath the surface allowing the plants to proliferate or multiply, like mint.

As I was researching the definition of root, I was amazed at the many figurative uses of the word. We speak of putting down roots when we plan to settle in a new location. Family roots represent the ancestry of a particular group of people. Roots metaphorically can have positive value; however, negative value may be assigned depending on the situation.

While I was pondering these botanical and literary connections, my heart wandered to the images that are found in Scripture. For instance, the phrase "For the love of money is a root of all kinds of evil," (1 Timothy 6:10) comes to mind. Or the fate of the seedlings that sprouted quickly, but had no soil in which to establish roots; those poor dears withered away. The Scriptures warn against allowing a root of bitterness to develop in our relationships (Hebrews 12:15).

One of the more positive images is of a firmly planted tree whose roots seek out the cool refreshing water of the nearby stream (Jeremiah 17:8). My favorite comparison is the believer being established in Christ. He is the source and origin of our life, and to be rooted in Him stabilizes our faith. I have seen huge trees uprooted by hurricane force winds. But I know that as believers deeply rooted in Christ, we will be able to survive the strong winds this life blows our way. And even if it feels like we are being bent to the end of our strength; Christ's roots are straining to strengthen the hold of His love on our lives.

Sabotage
an act or process tending to hamper or hurt; deliberate subversion[30]

Be self-controlled and alert. Your enemy the devil prowls around like a roaring lion looking for someone to devour. Resist him, standing firm in the faith, because you know that your brothers throughout the world are undergoing the same kind of sufferings.
1 Peter 5:8-9

Getting back to writing lately has evaded me. Spring break arrived earlier than most of the schools in our area. The cloudy, coldness of the week hampered any hopes of enjoying the outdoors. No time at the park or zoo for us. Instead my two teenage sons and I decided to rent a bazillion movies reverting to our vegetable states. Movies became the theme of our week. We went to the dollar show one day. Then boys went to see another movie on their own. Pathetic.

More dreary weather prevailed over Easter weekend. Just when I thought I'd get back on track the next Monday, the stomach virus came to visit; my son and then me. Being out of commission gave me some time to read and ponder.

What does one do when she has extra time on her hands? Get out her dictionary, silly! At least that's what this girl does. For some reason, yet undiscovered, I like to know what things mean. In a good sense I develop greater understanding, but this quest for meaning frustrates me, especially when I can't figure out life. Although, I strive to be a know-it-all, in reality I never will know it all. Only God is all-knowing and He's the One I must learn to trust with the unknowable aspects of my life.

Sabotage. Why does this word come to mind? I have an idea what it means, and sometimes I sabotage my own life. In my quest for meaning and purpose, I have discovered that God created me with meaning. He is the giver of purpose. I want to live out my life with the freedom that Christ secured at the cross. He has provided spiritual weapons to aid me in this spiritual battle, such as prayer and the Word. Yet, I allow thoughts into my mind that are opposed to the truth.

The source of these thoughts often can be attributed to our enemy, the father of lies. He is out to kill, steal and destroy every truth that has been revealed to us concerning our relationship with God. (John 10:10). His aim is to sabotage our very lives by various methods, including self-doubt. His cunning lies attack our belief about God and ourselves.

Remember Eve! It was the cunning of the serpent who led her astray. Paul warns the believers that deception comes through the mind, "But I am afraid that just as Eve was deceived by the serpent's cunning, your minds may somehow be led astray from your sincere and pure devotion to Christ" (2 Corinthians 11: 3). The battlefield is in the mind. How hard this concept is to get through my thick head. I try to keep my mind focused on the Prince of Peace, then boom some bad weather over Spring break, a trying day or bad health throws me off. I am vulnerable. Thoughts of worthlessness and despair besiege me. An all out war is being waged against me. What am I to do? I really can't do anything.

God overcomes my despair with His Word, with His wooing Holy Spirit who prompts me to pick up one of my devotion books. Then, bam! God counterattacks, rescues and provides the way out in the midst of the sabotage.

Often it seems like the enemy is on a serious campaign to keep me from living the freedom that I have gained in Christ (Galatians 5:1). I see in my own life hindrances to stay on track with the tasks and opportunities God has laid before me. Once I decide to make some inroads regarding discipline in my life, then hindrances start bombarding me daily, slowing me down and making progress difficult. Old thought patterns and negative thinking return with a vengeance. I thought I threw off those entanglements. I thought spring would be my salvation from the winter blahs. But God says, "No! I am your light and your salvation. Make me, the stronghold of your life!" (Psalm 27:1)

God is shedding light on my wrong thinking about the seasons. I think one season will rescue me from another. I tend to love one season more than another. My heart seeks fulfillment in a certain time of the year, instead of resting in the love of God, enjoying His presence through each season as its intended purpose works itself out in my daily life. I look forward to beginnings and can't wait for some things to end. I think there is a connection to my literal struggle with the passing seasons each year, and the seasons or stages of my life. I am trying to recreate old seasons and experiences. But God wants me to enjoy the moment.⋖

Surrender

to give oneself up into the power of another [31]

> *This is what the Sovereign LORD, the Holy One of Israel, says: "In repentance and rest is your salvation, in quietness and trust is your strength, but you would have none of it."*
> *Isaiah 30:15*

> *"The trees were beautiful this weekend in the country and each one had its own beauty, I thought-now look at that splendor-and to think that God loves me more than these… and they go through change, they surrender their leaves every year in a cycle that takes them from glory to greater glory, only to seemingly die before they are new again in even greater beauty, growing year by year."*
> *Kelly Greer*

The above quote was written by one of my dear friends in response to a conversation we were having via e-mail regarding how we each respond to changes. The next day, I pondered on the front porch, while watching the red maple shed its leaves. I marveled at how easily the tree surrendered its beautiful leaves. Do I hear it complaining that God took away what the tree worked so hard on all year? Does it argue that those were its best leaves yet? Does it resent having to give them up? Does the tree bend over and try to reattach that which has already served its purpose? Of course not, yet how often I have languished over the seasonal changes of my life. I wanted to cling to the memories of days gone by, instead of rejoicing in each new day. I have suffocated my children with my hovering, because I am not ready to let them go. I have tried to recreate past experiences in order to hang on just a little longer to the beauty of those moments. Yet, God's mercies are new every morning, and He desires me to yield to His love and plan for each fresh day, season or year.

I looked at the tree and saw its branches reaching like arms to the heavens, and I observed a picture of pure surrender. Raising my hands to the LORD in worship, I experienced a posture that was so fulfilling and freeing. While my arms were in the air, I abandoned the fallen leaves of my life at my feet. My heart was occupied with loving Him, instead of worrying about the mess around me that only He restores.

Another day that week I chatted on the phone with a friend. She bemoaned the chore of raking leaves, "It's so hard, I just get some raked up, and then another burst of wind sends more leaves to cover the ground." We dispose of the leaves to give an appearance of orderliness and accomplishment, when in reality we need to let the fallen leaves decay and do the work they were sent for. Fallen leaves can protect the grass from the harsh frosts. When they decompose they feed the yard. How often I fight the natural debris of living that God wants to use for my growth and protection.

The word surrender implies giving up a struggle after fighting to retain something. God knows us well. He provides the way out, yet we often refuse to take it. Can we not be more like a tree in autumn? Let's return to God and rest in His work in our lives, in so doing we will see deliverance from all kinds of calamities.

Instead of scurrying around, let's calm down and trust God because this will be our true strength. Just like the trees releasing their leaves at the force of the wind, so we must relinquish our lives to the strong gusts of the Spirit.

Time
an opportune or suitable moment[32]

*Be very careful, then, how you live-not as unwise but as
wise, making the most of every opportunity,
because the days are evil.
Ephesians 5:15-16*

On a recent walk I was surprised, as Father Time rode by on his bike. I always thought time just marched on, but actually he must ride a bike once in awhile. I saw him with my own eyes. Near the end of my walk he pedaled back past me and said, "Have a good day." I acknowledged him with a nod. Walking toward home with a happy heart, because I had met with Father Time and he had spoken to me. Lest you think I have gone totally bonkers, this really did happen. A man in my neighborhood with a white beard rode past me, and printed on the back of his green t-shirt were the words: "Father Time."

In our hectic lives we often wonder if we have enough time to get everything done. Catching up from one trip and getting ready for another, I was beginning to panic because I didn't have enough time to get everything done. The bike encounter reminded me that time is always moving, and I probably never will have enough time, but I really should enjoy the time I do have. Things always fall into place. Whenever I remember that my times are in our Heavenly Father's hands, then my schedule and my heart lighten up (Psalm 31:15). Sometimes I don't like what has to be put aside, but in the long run there is a time for everything.

We had a bunch of errands to run to get ready for our family vacation. I took the boys to get haircuts. After that we headed out on a spur of the moment shopping adventure. We ended up at the thrift store, and my very interesting sons began a quest for western wear for our trip to the Rocky Mountains, informing me they would be sporting their duds on the train ride between Durango and Silverton. One found a plaid flannel shirt to wear with his jeans and a cowboy hat. The other snagged a matching vest and pants, which reminded him of the old-time clerks of yesteryear. Their desire to dress their part, and enjoy themselves no matter what others may think of them prompted me to come up with this saying: "Life is a performance, so get your costume on, and ham it up." Those boys (young men, really) keep me smiling.

There are so many things that make life worth living, but there is One who is worth living life for, and that is the Lord Jesus Christ. He has set before us choices and promises, which if we allow will bring fulfillment to our lives. And He has given His life for us. (Romans 5:8). So live it up today, my friends. We have time, as long as God gives us breath. For now, I am off to buy myself a cowgirl hat, in order to participate in our adventure out west.∽

Unruly
not readily ruled, disciplined, or managed[33]

*Now the earth was formless and empty,
darkness was over the surface of the deep,
and the Spirit of God was hovering over the waters.
Genesis 1:2*

*"Move, I pray Thee, upon my disordered heart."
A Puritan Prayer*

Wrestling with an inner conflict, which I was having difficulty defining, found me reaching for my dictionary. I wasn't necessarily depressed, and not really sad; although maybe a bit tired. But I just couldn't pin this feeling down into an easily explained category. One of the hazards of being a definition enthusiast is that I am not happy unless I know what something means.

During this time of frustration, I came across the prayer quoted above. I had never really heard of a disordered heart before, but the phrase seemed to fit, and the Holy Spirit invited me to look a little closer at what this might have to do with me presently. Dictionary quest, here I come. Disordered was related to the word unruly which lead to my favorite subject discipline, or the lack thereof.

Discipline is a troublesome topic for me. I can't quite figure it out. Is it my friend or a nuisance? God's word says that when He disciplines us, it is out of His love for us (Revelation 3:19). And His discipline is not just a hasty judgment; it is for our benefit and a thorough examination regarding the condition of our heart.

Praying for the Spirit of God to move upon my disordered heart was a cry for Him to bring order to the chaos of my thoughts. I don't know about you, but I can get quite carried away with an onslaught of various thoughts. My mental to do list, anxiety about upcoming events, and concern over those I love and care for add up to a desire to just shut down. It is a chore to move forward, to do the next thing. The joy seeps out of things that usually buoy me up.

At first glance the phrase disordered heart brought to mind a messy room, something that needs to be restored to order. My tendency when a room is messy is to either close the door, as in the case of my teen-aged sons' rooms or if it's my clutter, I may overlook it until a later time when I just can't stand it anymore. When I do tackle the piles of junk or unfolded clothes that have gone untouched for days, it takes more time and effort than I really wanted to give the tasks.

A disordered heart takes more than my puny efforts to set it right. I often try to rearrange my time so as to incorporate spiritual activities into my life just to feel better about myself. Yet lasting change is accomplished by the One who moved over the face of the earth and created light and beauty out of darkness and chaos.

In my distress I contemplated the work of the Holy Spirit to restore inner peace. I was reminded that one of God's most powerful instruments, which He uses for discerning the state of my heart and mind, was His word. (Hebrews 4:12). Favorite verses began to flood my mind causing my thoughts to be reigned in under the unsurpassed calm that only the Lord can provide (Isaiah 26:3). I am ever grateful for His gentle, yet firm discipline in my life that leads to a harvest of righteousness and peace (Hebrews 12:11). The words of God and the Holy Spirit moved upon my disordered heart in a fresh expression of God's loving discipline.

Walk
to pursue a course of action or way of life[34]

*Blessed are those who have learned to acclaim you,
who walk in the light of your presence, O LORD.
Psalm 89:15*

After writing my Christmas list and checking it twice, I plopped into my chair. Then I asked myself the perennial question: "Why do I disrupt my whole life and rearrange my home for this holiday?" Jesus was definitely worth my undivided attention, but why so much frenzy just now. I wish I could say that I took the revolutionary step of just leaving my furniture arranged in its usual array and that I left the decorations in the attic. The tree sparkles in the corner, each room shimmers with holiday wonder, and the furniture has been moved to accommodate this seasonal display. I sigh with hopes of enjoying some quiet, reflective moments savoring the Savior.

Often I decorate with the colors, silver and gold, so I was intrigued when I came upon Peter's words in Acts, "Silver or gold I do not have, but what I have I give you" (Acts 3:6a). I may not be short on finances or physical health. Yet I often feel crippled by circumstances. Especially at this time of year, overwhelmed with expectations, I feel paralyzed. The offer of Peter to the crippled man seemed like an invitation to me: "In the name of Jesus of Nazareth, walk" (Acts 3:6b). To be able to walk with joy instead of dread would be a great thing to add to my Christmas list.

I believe the richest treasure God offered is the Name of Jesus. The power and hope of His reputation and promises fill me with joy, His very presence in me through His Holy Spirit. The result in the man's life when Peter invoked the Name beckons me. His ability to walk was regained. I need this kind of healing in my spirit, which becomes crippled by doubts and fears.

One morning, I woke up thinking about a situation that seemed hopeless. Then I remembered Abraham, who believed God for the impossible. That recollection prompted me to pray about the situation in light of God's character, in the name of Jesus. When I recall God's faithfulness to His own character my hope increases.

God's first creative act revealed His ability to make something out of nothing. In Genesis, we see God working with a formless, void and darkened situation. He spoke and light became a reality. The simple phrase, "Let there be" testified to God's ability to call into being that which does not exist. If God was able to call into being that which does not exist in former times, imagine what can He do now? He is still the same. He can still speak, and say "Let there be."

We have traveled a bit from Peter's offer, yet I want to end with him in mind. Remembering that we have much to gain and offer as a result of the Savior's gift. His very own life, which began in a manger. We can expect Christ to restore our spiritual ability to walk with God. What great celebration as we go forth praising God. Rich hope resounded through poor Peter's offer. Even if I have no earthly consolation, I do have the riches of Jesus. Jesus restored strong legs to a crippled man, thus He can revive my faltering spirit.

Others will marvel at God's healing love in our lives. Although we may not have silver or gold, we can offer Christ's gift of salvation that produces an abundance of peace, hope and love.

Wet
still moist enough to smudge or smear[35]

If we claim to be without sin, we deceive ourselves and the truth is not in us. If we confess our sins, he is faithful and just and will forgive us our sins and purify us from all unrighteousness. If we claim we have not sinned, we make him out to be a liar and his word has no place in our lives.
1 John 1:8-10

One beautiful morning while out walking our dog, I noticed the road was marked off by traffic cones. A small backhoe was parked at the corner. I happened to be walking on the sidewalk, which is unusual as I tend to walk on the road (Must be a left over habit from growing up a country girl). As I approached the corner, absorbed in the praise song on my i-Pod, I let the dog and my feet carry me down the sidewalk. I noticed a metal bar over the sidewalk, stepped right over it and began to sink— in wet cement.

I stepped out of the cement and urged our dog to follow along. Once we were out I decided to walk on the road. As we neared the end of the street, I spotted a crew working on the sidewalk. I debated whether or not to confess my blunder. I confessed hoping that it was not too late for the crew to erase the evidence of our footprints in the cement. They thanked me for telling them, and assured me that most people do not, which, of course, ruins their work. I was glad that I had confessed.

This little adventure prompted me to question the times I had noticed the danger signs of a sinful choice, but just ignored them, walking directly into sin. God delights in our repentance and our quick confession. He forgives us and corrects the mess we've created.

I thought about what would have happened if I hadn't admitted my error to the workers. The evidence would be permanently set in the concrete. Not to mention the time and money it would take to repair the sidewalk.

What an incentive to confess to God without delay, when we realize we've stepped astray.

Notes

_____

[1] "apt." *Merriam-Webster.com*. 2011. http://www.merriam-webster.com (9 Sept 2011).

[2] "beloved."Ibid.

[3] "blessed." Ibid.

[4] "change." Ibid.

[5] "choose." Ibid.

[6] "clarity." Ibid.

[7] "cram." Ibid.

[8] "cure." Ibid.

[9] "define." Ibid.

[10] "deliver." Ibid.

[11] "ending." Ibid.

[12] "epiphany." Ibid.

[13] "expect." Ibid.

[14] "focus." Ibid.

[15] "gospel." Ibid.

[16] "home." Ibid.

[17] "hope." Ibid.

[18] "husbandry." Ibid.

[19] "husband." Ibid.

[20] "bower." Ibid.

[21] "journey." Ibid.

[22] "love." Ibid.

[23] "new." Ibid.

[24] "persevere." Ibid.

[25] "cadenza." Ibid.

[26] "residue." Ibid.

[27] "resist." Ibid.

[28] "retreat." Ibid.

[29] "root." Ibid.

[30] "sabotage." Ibid.

[31] "surrender." Ibid.

[32] "time." Ibid.

[33] "unruly." Ibid.

[34] "walk." Ibid.

[35] "wet." Ibid.

Kel Rohlf lives in St. Louis, MO with her husband of twenty-five years, and their two sons.

To read more musings on the Word and words from Kel, check out her blog:

Nourishment for the Soul: A Place to Feed on Words

www.nourishsoul.blogspot.com